ROME
THEN & NOW

ROME
THEN & NOW

FEDERICA D'ORAZIO

THUNDER BAY
P·R·E·S·S

San Diego, California

Thunder Bay Press
An imprint of the Advantage Publishers Group
THUNDER BAY 5880 Oberlin Drive, San Diego, CA 92121-4794
P · R · E · S · S   www.thunderbaybooks.com

Produced by Salamander Books,
an imprint of Anova Books Company Ltd.,
10 Southcombe Street, London, W14 0RA, United Kingdom

© 2007 Salamander Books

All notations of errors or omissions should be addressed to Thunder Bay Press,
Editorial Department, at the above address. All other correspondence (author
inquiries, permissions) concerning the content of this book should be addressed
to Salamander Books, 10 Southcombe Street, London, W14 0RA, U.K.

ISBN-13: 978-1-59223-831-6
ISBN-10: 1-59223-831-9

The Library of Congress has cataloged the original Thunder Bay edition as follows:
D'Orazio, Federica, 1971–
    Rome then and now / Federica D'Orazia.
      p. cm.
      ISBN 1-59223-292-2
      1. Rome (Italy)--History--Pictorial works. I. Title.

DG806.8.D67 2004
945'.63'00222--dc22

                                                  2004049751

1 2 3 4 5 11 10 09 08 07
Printed in China

ACKNOWLEDGMENTS
Special thanks to my husband Alessandro Cianchi, Professor Ferruccio Di Cori,
Franchina Finocchio, and Cesare and Vilma Cianchi for their memories and direct
experience; to Laura Larcan and Enrico Galasso for the agenda of cultural events of
Rome and technical assistance. Many thanks for the helpful assistance of Dr. Laura
Biancini, Director of the Ceccarius Fund at the National Library; thanks also for the
invaluable assistance of Dr. Fabio Betti from the photo archive at Museo di Roma.

Federica D'Orazio's website is www.guidaturisticaroma.it.

PICTURE CREDITS
The publisher wishes to thank the following for kindly supplying the photographs
that appear in this book:

"Then" photography
© Museo di Roma / Archivio Fotografico Comunale 6, 8, 14, 18, 20, 22, 24, 26, 36,
46, 52, 54, 58, 62, 68, 72, 74, 76, 82, 86, 92, 94, 96, 104, 106, 108, 112, 118, 122,
130, 132, 142. © Fondo Ceccarius / Biblioteca Nazionale Centrale di Roma 12, 16,
44, 48, 70, 78, 84, 98, 102, 116, 124, 136. © CORBIS 80. © Bettmann/CORBIS 32,
38, 40, 60, 88, 138. © Michael Maslan Historic Photographs/CORBIS 50. © Istituto
Centrale per il Catalogo e la Documentazione 1, 10, 28, 30, 34, 42, 56, 66, 64, 90,
100, 110, 114, 120, 126, 128, 134, 140.

"Now" photography
All photographs taken by David Watts with the exception of © Dallas and John
Heaton/CORBIS 33. Page 105 courtesy of Alessandro Cianchi.

For cover photo credits, please see back flap of cover.

All inquiries regarding images should be addressed to Anova Books Company Ltd.

INTRODUCTION

Rome is like an old lady once aristocratic, but today living in slightly reduced circumstances. I am immensely proud to have been born here, because inside of these walls, covered by moss, ivy, and vine, live the most beautiful expressions of art and architecture that have been left to posterity.

There is so much history in Rome that to fully appreciate the city, an understanding of early Rome is essential. According to tradition, Rome was founded on April 21 in the year 753 BC. Legend has it that Romulus and Remus, the twin sons of Mars, the god of war, were cast adrift on the river Tiber and raised by a she-wolf. After killing his brother in a family feud, Romulus later carved out the boundaries of the *Roma Quadrata* on the Palatine Hill to the east of the Tiber.

Romulus became the first king of Rome, but after seven kings the citizens of Rome rebelled and in 510 BC they formed their own government of the people: the Roman republic. Indeed, the word "republic" comes from the Latin *res publica* (matters of state). Although the city was sacked in 390 BC by the Gaul tribes, over the years the Roman army gradually took control of Italy, wresting power from the Etruscans, the Carthaginians, and the Greeks.

But it was the Roman general Julius Caesar who changed the face of the city. After conquering Gaul (modern-day France) in 51 BC, he advanced his legions on Rome. When he crossed the river Rubicon, dividing his own province from Italy, it was an act of war from which there was no returning. Caesar defeated his Roman enemies, but he was famously murdered in 44 BC by senators angered by his seizure of power. It was to be another twenty years before his adopted son, Octavian, established authority as the first Roman emperor, Augustus Caesar. Another eighty-six emperors would rule until the fall of Rome to the Visigoths in AD 476. At its height in AD 117, under the emperor Trajan, the Romans controlled most of Europe, Asia Minor, Egypt, and north Africa.

A good way to get to know modern-day Rome is to get lost in the narrow streets of the city center and look up at the street names. The names conjure up the ancient trades, historic buildings, leading citizens, and the most important dates in the city's history. You'll find some of these dates inscribed: September 20, 1870, the end of the popes' rule and the date of the annexation of Rome to Italy; April 25, 1944, the liberation of Italy in World War II; June 2, 1946, the birth of the Republic of Italy; and the most beloved by the Romans, April 21, 753 BC, the founding of the city.

Wandering around the colorful and lively streets, it is sometimes hard to see the ancient city hiding beneath the modern one. Via di Grottapinta, a street east of Campo de'Fiori, follows the curves of the ancient Theater of Pompeii; the Church of Santa Maria Sopra Minerva has been built on top of a former temple; the Piazza Navona follows the shape of the Stadium of Domitian; and the Piazza della Republica follows the *exedra* (discussion house) of the emperor Diocletian.

Things change slowly under the Roman sun and still Rome is divided into the *rioni* (ancient wards), originally set down by Emperor Augustus and surviving to this day. On older streets, there are symbols of the wards and one will see small travertine plaques with odd symbols such as columns, angels, and pinecones.

Looking at the traffic congestion today, it is hard to imagine that until a few years ago the city's population was not that of a major capital. In 1870 the city numbered only 200,000 inhabitants, all living within the perimeter of the Aurelian Wall, and had large agricultural areas that allowed the city to grow its own food. Many of the historical photographs in this book bear testimony to this, with cultivated crops and herded animals around areas that today are the preserve of tourists.

In 1870 Rome became the new capital of Italy—buildings were demolished and streets were opened up to make traveling around the city easier. At the same time the big parks of the aristocratic families and the arable land were swallowed up, while the area around the Termini Railway Station and Via Veneto underwent major renovations. The new face of the city created a mood of change: ghettos were demolished and embankments were strengthened to keep floods from the river Tiber from laying more silt among the ancient ruins and raising the ground level, as it had done over the years.

From 1929 to 1931 the Fascist dictator Benito Mussolini isolated ancient sites and buildings, creating the Foro Italico sports complex. Today there are still some *fasci littori* (symbols of the Fascists) too deeply carved in the marble to be erased.

During the period of Fascist rule, the city had a million inhabitants, but after 1945 the population grew, particularly in the suburbs, and now almost four million people live in Rome—with only 125,000 of those making their home in the city center.

For the year 2000, considered a holy year by many Romans, much was done to improve the city, from the restyling of the Termini Railway Station to the restoration of many historic monuments. Planners reduced the congestion in the city center by introducing limited-traffic zones, and transformed Via Fori Imperiali and the Appian Way, which became pedestrian areas on Sundays.

Rome is also a place of contradictions: there are two states in the city, the Italian and the Vatican. The Vatican is the smallest state in the world, but it has the largest congregation, the Roman Catholic faith. Although only 3 percent of the population goes to church, the Vatican still has a profound influence on the Italian government and the country's laws.

Italy has changed dramatically in the last two millennia, but Rome, the "Eternal City," has changed little. This is why Romans enjoy saying to tourists, "If I am the dream you wish to change into reality, here I am . . . to stay."

On Easter Sunday, 1870, several months before Rome was captured and annexed to Italy by Giuseppe Garibaldi, all the wealthy families faithful to the pope met in the Piazza St. Peter for his last blessing and to pray for the uncertain future of the Vatican state. In this picture one can see the many carriages that occupied the piazza and the awning used to cover the balcony in order to amplify the voice of the pope and to offer protection from the weather. The top of the colonnade is ringed with 140 statues of saints. Created by Gian Lorenzo Bernini between 1656 and 1667, it almost matches the Colosseum in size and grandeur.

Today the pedestrianized piazza, with its 67,000 square yards of space, can hold crowds in excess of 60,000. The line of travertine stone around the colonnade marks the borders of the Vatican state. Although only 108 acres in total, the Vatican houses a heliport, post office, train station, radio station, newspaper, pharmacy, and a hundred Swiss guards. Each day, 20,000 people visit St. Peter's Basilica—one of the largest in the world—and its immense treasures such as the *Pietà*, created by Michelangelo when he was just twenty-three years old. The holiest places in the Vatican are the tomb of St. Peter under the main altar—decorated with ninety-five lamps— and the tombs of 147 of the 266 popes of the Catholic church. A papal audience is held every Wednesday morning, and every Sunday the pope salutes visitors from the windows of his apartment, seen here on the right of the piazza.

Named after Pope Pius X and decorated with a fountain built by Pius IX, the piazza was at the head of the *borghi* (quarters) in front of the Piazza St. Peter. The borghi were districts created by Anglo-Saxon kings and pilgrims who came to visit the grave of St. Peter.

Leo IV built walls around the borghi as a protection against barbarian invasions after it was pillaged by the Saracens in 846. The walls also served the function of connecting the Vatican palaces to the fortress of the popes, Castle St. Angelo.

This particular area was partly demolished by Mussolini in 1936 to create a boulevard called Via della Conciliazione. To create this wide street, some historical palaces were demolished; however, a few can still be found here. These include the Palazzo del St. Uffizio, once known as the center of the Roman Inquisition; the Palazzo dei Convertendi, where the artist Raphael died (allegedly of syphilis) in 1520 at the age of thirty-seven; and the beautiful Palazzo dei Penitenzieri with its amazing fifteenth-century frescoes and which survives today as a restaurant. From 1958, classical concerts were held in the auditorium of St. Cecilia in the Palazzo Pio but have recently moved to the beautiful, modern Music Park auditorium—a structure designed by the architect Renzo Piano and located in the Flaminio district.

The river Tiber, which up until the twentieth century frequently burst its banks, depositing silt on nearby houses, has played a key role in Rome's history. A settlement was established here in the Iron Age because it was an easy place to cross the river. In the eighteenth century, the Tiber was rich with fish and the water was so clean that the people, believing it to be curative, would drink it. The building on the right of this 1900 photograph is Castle St. Angelo, which was built on the mausoleum of the emperor Adrian and then transformed into the fortress of the popes. The statues decorating the top of the mausoleum were thrown at the marauding Goths during a siege in 537. The castle was linked to the Vatican by a corridor running along the top of the Leonine Wall. Part of the castle was a notorious prison; its place in classical music is firmly established, as it features as a backdrop to the opera *Tosca* by Puccini. The bridge across the Tiber is known as the Bridge of Angels and was restyled in the seventeenth century by Gian Lorenzo Bernini.

Today no one comes to Rome to fish in the Tiber or drink its water for curative reasons. Tourists can traverse its ancient course in small ferryboats that stop at the main bridges, of which Rome has twenty-eight in total. A tradition of diving from the Cavour, the bridge that precedes the St. Angelo bridge, has become a New Year's Day tradition for the courageous. In 1888 embankments were created to protect the city from floods, and buildings facing the river were demolished. The castle is now a fascinating museum with breathtaking views of the city. Behind its austere facade, beautiful painted halls dating from the Renaissance can be found. During the summer, the gardens of the castle host book fairs and—unsurprisingly, given its musical connection—classical concerts.

Via del Corso has existed since ancient times. Originally it was named Via Lata (Wide Street) and was considered the main street of Rome, the entrance for the many visitors coming from the north through Porta Flaminia, or Porta del Popolo. During the Renaissance it assumed its present dimensions. In 1466 Pope Paul II moved the famous Roman Carnival here, with the race of the horses which gave the name Corso (Race) to the street. The event, which started in Piazza del Popolo and ended in Piazza Venezia, was abolished in 1882, shortly before this photograph was taken, after a tragic accident. Flanking the street are the houses of Roman high society, whose residents could see the race directly from their balconies. The first building on the left is Palazzo Bonaparte, which was at one time home to the mother of Napoleon.

The street is now the main shopping street in Rome and it is almost a mile long. Some of the aristocratic palaces are now museums that house temporary art exhibitions or the offices for large banks. One of the streets perpendicular to the Corso is the elegant Via Condotti, the Fifth Avenue of Rome. The street numbering on Via del Corso follows the old system of the city: starting on one side of the road, the numbers originate from Piazza del Popolo, head toward Piazza Venezia, and then return on the other side of the road, until they reach Piazza del Popolo again.

The imposing ruins of the Stadium of Domitian, which had held athletic competitions since AD 85, were slowly transformed into a square that retained the elongated shoe shape of the stadium. In the seventeenth century, Pope Innocent X Pamphili, who owned a palace in the piazza, commissioned Francesco Borromini to build the Church of St. Agnes in Agone while commissioning Borromini's rival, Bernini, to build the Fountain of the Four Rivers in the Piazza Navona. An amusing story about the rivalry between the two architects claims that the statue representing the Ganges raised his arm to protect himself from the church's collapse, while the one representing the Nile covered his head to avoid the dreadful sight. The piazza was used as a fruit and vegetable market, and between 1652 and 1866 it was flooded each Saturday in August to create an artificial lake.

The square is still very pleasant today with its popular cafés and restaurants. It is one of the widest squares in Rome. During the liberation of Italy by the Allied forces, the piazza was used as a camp for the soldiers, who took home the fingers of the statues as souvenirs. There is a famous toy fair held here each winter, culminating on January 6 with the Roman feast of Befana, an old magical woman who gives presents to the good children and sugared charcoal to the bad ones. Rome's city planners are now devising an elaborate system of lights to illuminate the masterpieces of Bernini and Borromini.

Some of the merchants from the old fruit and vegetable market set up their stalls near the Fountain of Moor. The fountain, shown here in 1867, was designed by Bernini and stands at the southern end of the piazza, opposite what was then a relatively modest area of houses and apartments. This picture also shows the Renaissance Church of San Giacomo degli Spagnoli, assigned to the Spanish community by Pope Alexander VI in the sixteenth century after many Spaniards had moved to the Church of St. Maria di Monserrato. The facade was deprived of its Baroque decorations, while the interior was divested of its marble ornaments. The nearby Palazzo Braschi was the home of the Italian Fascists led by Mussolini.

The church, bought by a French religious order in 1878, is now called Nostra Signora del Sacro Cuore. The upper part of the church was completed in 1888. In the 1930s the apse of the church was removed and rebuilt for the Corso del Rinascimento. Today the area is one of the most elegant and expensive to live in, with houses of VIPs and politicians, as well as the famous Christie's auction house. Today the beautiful and now peaceful Palazzo Braschi is the Museum of Rome, with an impressive collection of paintings showing Rome in former times. Close by is the "talking statue" of Pasquino, once used to express the voice of the poor about the government of the popes. People would hang placards containing defiant messages around the neck of the statue. Today it is still used as a means of speaking out against government policies.

The Piazza St. Andrea della Valle, found just off the Piazza Navona, is named after the valley and lake that the emperor Nero was reputed to have sailed across in his golden ship. Built in 1591, the church has the tallest dome after St. Peter's and it is one of the main counterreformation churches of the sixteenth century, with works of art by Borromini, Domenichino, and Lanfranco. One of the first scenes in the opera *Tosca* by Giacomo Puccini was set here. The church, shown here in 1872, overlooked the narrow streets leading to the Piazza Navona and the Palazzo Madama, the house of the senate.

Today the church overlooks a much wider street. The building opposite was demolished in Mussolini's time to create a faster link between the center of Rome and the Prati quarter near the Vatican. The name Rinascimento (Renaissance) no longer reflects the overall style of this street. The white palace at the head of the street was built in 1937 and on the facade was placed a thin she-wolf with abundant mammaries—the symbol of Rome and its founder, Romulus—which were later prudishly reduced. Fortunately, the most historical palaces on the street were saved, such as the Church of St. Ivo alla Sapienza, by Borromini, and the Palazzo Madama, designed by Raphael.

This image of Piazza della Chiesa Nuova shows the Oratory of St. Philip Neri (right), built in 1572 by Gregory XIII and Cardinal Cesi for the followers of St. Philip. It was designed by Martino Longhi the Elder and restored in 1637 by Borromini. In the oratory, St. Philip started the musical gatherings known as *oratorios*, which then lent their name to a new form of musical composition. The oratory is attached to the Church of St. Maria in Vallicella, which locals still call Chiesa Nuova (New Church).

Many areas surrounding the Piazza Navona were demolished between 1883 and 1888. The Fontana della Terrina in the middle of the square was moved here from the Campo dei Fiori in 1925. In the Chiesa Nuova are several masterpieces by Baroque painters, including one by Rubens. Today the oratory is used for conferences and a variety of cultural activities. It also houses the Vallicelliana Library, one of the first Italian libraries to open to the public, and the Capitoline Museum, which includes a collection of Roman newspapers dating back to the eighteenth century.

This area combined two diverse aspects of Rome: the sacred and the profane. Although it was the site of the Vatican offices, it was also the area associated with partisan fighting by those arguing for and against the unification of Italy. This is the only piazza in Rome without a church, and Puccini's nationalistic opera *Tosca* was set here. This photograph shows the inauguration of the statue of the philosopher Giordano Bruno on June 9, 1889. Bruno was burned by the Catholic church as a heretic in the year 1600. His ideas about an endless universe with no center were not shared by the church. Although the piazza is named after a field of flowers that once covered the site, it has long been at the heart of the city as a site associated with public executions and protests.

This popular fruit, vegetable, and fish market, originally in the Piazza
Navona, has been held here since 1869. It is also a lively place at
night, known for its pizzerias and other inexpensive restaurants. In
the basement of the Costanza restaurant it is possible to see parts of
the Theater of Pompeii, the ancient theater where Julius Caesar was
killed on the Ides of March in 44 BC.

Cardinal Alessandro Farnese built his palace here in the sixteenth century. The Palazzo Farnese is considered the most beautiful Renaissance palace in Rome. The building, pictured here in 1864, took a staggering seventy-five years to complete. Michelangelo contributed to it, and part of the palace was built using marble recycled from the Colosseum. At either end of the piazza are two huge granite basins, moved here from the Baths of Caracalla, which were converted into fountains in 1626. Above the door on the facade is the coat of arms of the prince of Borbone, an exile here after the annexation of Naples to Italy.

The Palazzo Farnese has housed the French embassy since 1874 and France still has to pay a symbolic rent of a few euros until 2035. Unfortunately, the outstanding collection of statues was moved to Naples when one of the Farnese family married the prince of Naples. The collection is now in the National Archaeological Museum and the Museum of Capodimonte in Naples. During the summer this area is often transformed into an open arena for showing movies. The palazzo also houses a very good collection of art and archaeology and the public is awarded rare glimpses of some beautiful Baroque paintings, including those of Annibale Carracci, when it is opened for public viewing.

When this picture was taken in 1872, this piazza was named Piazza Cesarini after the Palazzo Cesarini. In the middle of the piazza, a horse lies injured, surrounded by a small group of onlookers inspecting the accident. The area was also called "Calcarari" after the several kilns that were used to transform stone from the ancient ruins and statues into lime chalk. Some families saved statues from the kilns, buying them cheaply and using them as friezes or decorations for their gardens and courtyards. This explains why a lot of palaces in the area, like the Palazzo Mattei, are filled with ancient works of art.

Between 1926 and 1929 Mussolini made large-scale changes to the area. The Palazzo Cesarini was demolished and the area beneath it excavated, revealing four temples of the Roman republic. The temples were located next to the Theater of Pompeii, where Julius Caesar was killed in 44 BC. Today, in place of that ancient theater, one finds the Teatro Argentina, built in 1816, which staged the premiere of *The Barber of Seville* by Rossini. The piazza is now famous for the many wild cats living in its ruins, so many that an association was formed to take care of them.

The Rotunda is the popular name given to the Pantheon, a circular temple dedicated to the gods. The original Pantheon was built by Agrippa in the first century BC but was destroyed in a fire. It was then rebuilt by Emperor Hadrian in AD 118–125. It became a church in 609, dedicated to St. Mary of the Martyrs, and was rescued from the disrepair into which it had fallen. Its dome, at 141 feet in diameter, is the widest in Rome—the great Michelangelo didn't dare to build a wider dome;

St. Peter's Basilica is less than three feet smaller. In the seventeenth century, Gian Lorenzo Bernini added two belfries to "improve" the building. They were quickly ridiculed and became known as "ass's ears." The square in front was used as a market, especially for fish, until 1847. It is now infamous for the execution of a particular merchant who sold sausages made from human flesh. This photograph dates to 1880.

In 1883 the ass lost its ears as the belfries were demolished, along with the fence around the beautiful sixteenth-century fountain. The Pantheon is an obligatory stop for tourists for several reasons. Not only is it the best-preserved temple in Rome, but there are also many cafés surrounding the colorful piazza, selling the best ice cream and coffee in the area. Inside the Pantheon are the tombs of Italian kings, still guarded by monarchists loyal to the Savoy family, dressed in their blue uniforms. The most important tomb is that of Raphael, the genius of the Renaissance, who was buried here in 1520. When it rains in Rome, people come to the Pantheon to experience it: the circular opening in the dome is open to the elements.

This sight is one that has delighted tourists for centuries—refined visitors taking a grand tour of Europe could not miss the Trevi Fountain. The statues of Neptune and his court are surrounded by what is known as "virgin water." The legend says that, in the time of Octavian Augustus, the soldiers of Agrippa were exhausted on returning to Rome when a virgin pointed to a spring of water next to them. Agrippa then made the spring into an aqueduct that ended at this spot. In the seventeenth century, Pope Urban VIII decided to build a beautiful fountain here and increased the tax on wine to raise the money for the enterprise—and was consequently nicknamed "Papa Gabella" (the Taxing Pope). But it was not until 1732 that Pope Clement XII ordered work to be started on the fountain.

On first sight it is hard to believe anyone would create such a majestic fountain in such a small piazza. This is a fountain beloved by movie directors who have shot their films here, including *Three Coins in the Fountain* (Jean Negulesco, 1954) and *La Dolce Vita* (Federico Fellini, 1961). Recently restored, it is one of the most-photographed places in the city and is eternally popular because of the tradition of the three coins. The tradition is that one coin thrown in the fountain assures a return to Rome, two coins assures the love of a desired partner, and three coins secures a marriage. For years a few Romans took advantage of this tradition and came in the night to steal the money the tourists had thrown in, but now the money is collected by the city for charity. The building seen behind the fountain, Palazzo Poli, today houses a design museum that was recently reopened to the public.

In spite of its name, these steps were created by the architect Francesco de Sanctis between 1723 and 1726, with the use of French money. The Spanish name comes from the embassy that stands at the foot of the steps on the left-hand side of the piazza. It was rumored to be dangerous to pass too close to the embassy because a lot of people were being forced to join the Spanish army. The church at the top, Trinità dei Monti, belongs to French nuns and was built by the king of France, Charles VIII, in 1495. The steps were traditionally a place for flower sellers, often women from Ciociaria, an area south of Rome that was famous for its beautiful women who worked as artists' models.

Next to the church is one of the best hotels in Rome, the Hotel Hassler, where all the VIPs and Hollywood stars stay when in Rome. One can enjoy a breathtaking view from the Hassler's rooftop. Although the flower sellers were banned, the tradition of flowers is kept alive with azalea decorations covering the steps in the springtime. On the right of the steps is the Percy Bysshe Shelley and John Keats Memorial House. Further on the left is the house museum of the Italian surrealist painter Giorgio de Chirico. Each July, a fashion show is held on the steps, featuring the most glamorous names in the Italian fashion industry.

This column is located in the Piazza di Spagna, below the Scalinata di Spagna. It is next to the Barcaccia Fountain—a very sober, boat-shaped fountain commissioned by Pope Urban VIII and designed by the father-and-son team of Pietro and Gian Lorenzo Bernini. The column honors the Catholic celebration of the Immaculate Conception and was erected in 1857. The building just at the back of the column is the Propaganda Fide, created by Gian Lorenzo Bernini and his competitor, Borromini.

In the first years of the twentieth century, trams passed through here, but Mussolini disapproved of this form of transportation and many lines were abolished after he came to power in 1922. Every December 8, a legal holiday in Italy to celebrate the Immaculate Conception, the piazza is filled with people watching firemen crown the Madonna on the top of the column, a ceremony that is also attended by the pope. This piazza is very busy today with people passing to and from the Trevi Fountain.

Even at the turn of the century, when this photograph was taken, the signs in the stores of the elegant Via Condotti were written in English and French, a courtesy to the many international visitors who stayed in the area. At this time, the street was full of hotels—such as the Hotel d'Allemagne and the Hotel de Londres—and princes, poets, and writers such as Thackeray and Tennyson stayed here. The street was named for the *condotti* (lead pipes) of the aqueduct that feed the Trevi Fountain and also provide water to the Barcaccia Fountain, which was created in 1629 by the Bernini family—the father, Pietro, and his more famous son, Gian Lorenzo.

This area is now a famous and exclusive shopping district; Via Condotti is known as the "Fifth Avenue of Rome." There are stores selling the best labels in the Italian fashion and jewelry industries, including Armani, Valentino, Gucci, Bulgari, and Damiani. The street also boasts the famous Café Greco, which was founded by a Greek immigrant in 1760 and survives to this day. The café has many autographed pictures and interesting rooms that are dotted with statues, paintings, and drawings. It is said to be one of just three cafés in the world that are over 200 years old; the other two are in Venice and Paris.

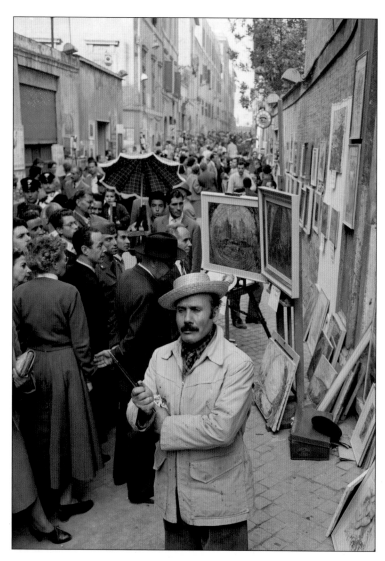

As the artistic center of Rome, since 1860 Via Margutta (shown here in 1954) has played host to a circle of artists who exhibited their canvases along the sidewalks. The street has attracted artists since the seventeenth century, many of whom had their studios here. The houses in the street often had balconies filled with flowers, and, to the rear, courtyard gardens. There were many art and antiques galleries occupying the ground floors. The first theater in Italy to use women in its performances was located on this street. In 1798, women replaced *castrati*—boys who were castrated to keep their voices intact—at the Vicolo d'Alibert. The initial performance drew a lot of men curious to see the actresses who, at that time, were considered to be on a par with prostitutes. It was seen as so outrageous that the castrati—possibly worried about their future careers—invaded the theater and stopped the play during the second act.

This is definitely one of the most charming and romantic streets of downtown Rome, just off the Spanish Steps. The groundbreaking theater no longer exists; it was destroyed by a fire and replaced, ironically, by a nunnery. The movie *Roman Holiday* was filmed here, with Gregory Peck living at No. 51; the avant-garde film director Federico Fellini and his wife, the actress Giulietta Masina, used to live at No. 109. Now the high cost of housing has sent the artists away. However, it is still fascinating to look at the galleries and at the stores that specialize in restoring furniture and making handicrafts. In June and October this peaceful street comes to life for the Margutta Art Exhibition, when artists display their works along the street, just as they did in the past.

On June 4, 1944, the Allied army entered Rome along Via Casilina while the Nazis escaped to the north. After twenty years of Fascism, World War II and the power of Mussolini were over—for Romans, at least. All over the city, the people greeted the soldiers as saviors, kissing them and passing them their children to be blessed. This photograph shows the soldiers leaving Via del Corso, between the "twin churches" of St. Maria di Montesanto and St. Maria dei Miracoli, having crossed through the city. Though Lieutenant General Mark Clark was cheered by the citizens of Rome, other Allied commanders were not so complimentary. They accused him of allowing the Germans time to retreat and regroup by taking a detour to liberate a city that the enemy had no plans to defend.

The Via del Corso is so famous that other main streets around Italy have also become known as "Corso." It is one of three streets that converge on the Piazza del Popolo and radiate from it like the three prongs of a trident: Via di Ripetta on the right, Via del Corso in the center, and Via del Babuino on the left. The two churches dedicated to St. Maria date from the seventeenth century.

The Orologio Idraulico (Hydraulic Clock) stands in the middle of Villa Borghese and was designed by a Dominican priest named Embriago for the 1867 Universal Exhibition in Paris. It shows the hour from each of its four sides and its water mechanism can be seen through a glass screen. The clock stands in the beautiful gardens laid out by Giuseppe Valadier in 1814, in a park previously owned by the Borghese family. They had to sell all their property at a low cost to the government because of the taxes they owed after the unification of Italy.

Today, Borghese Park is an attractive destination for walking, cycling, and sightseeing. The water mechanism is not as reliable as it once was and only by chance does it ever show the right time. The park is almost four miles in circumference and contains museums, such as the Borghese Gallery, a zoo, a children's movie theater, and a puppet theater. It also has a lake with rowboats for rent and a tethered air balloon for taking in panoramic views.

The Piazza Barberini, pictured here in 1860, was a busy residential area. The statue of Triton was created by Gian Lorenzo Bernini in 1640 for the Barberinis, the most powerful family in Rome, who lived in a grand house on the square. The bumblebees carved in detail on the fountain are the symbol of the family and can be found everywhere in the city.

Although grandiose in design, the fountain had a practical purpose: local women would wash clothes here and slap them dry against the posts surrounding the fountain. The gate on the far right was called "Il Portonaccio" (the Bad Gate) and was a secondary entrance to the Palazzo Barberini.

Today, in place of the gate there is Via Barberini, which is full of travel agencies and stores offering discount flights. To create the street, a 2,000-seat theater was demolished and the Barberini house was transformed into an art museum. Unfortunately, the beauty of this work of art has been compromised by its location in an area of heavy traffic, so it is difficult to stop and admire Bernini's creation. On the left is the beginning of Via Veneto—a fashionable street of restaurants, hotels, and cafés that is flanked by trees. At the beginning of the street is the noted Cemetery of the Capuchins. The low building behind the figure of Triton in the earlier photo has been replaced by the Hotel Bristol-Bernini.

The expansion of this street under the kings of Italy was one of the major projects that led to Rome's elevation as the capital city. On the left, at the beginning of the street, is the Bocconi store, built in the style of a French emporium with the innovative use of elevators and electric light produced by dynamos run from gas engines. In the 1920s, the name was changed to La Rinascente (the Renascent), which was suggested by the poet Gabriele D'Annunzio, who was paid well for the choice of name. The street takes its name from Bernini's statue in Piazza Barberini, where the street begins. The other stores have long canopies to protect their goods from the sun.

This street is still full of stores today; it links the city center with the northeastern suburbs and leads to the elegant Via Veneto. La Rinascente still stands, one side facing Via del Corso and the other facing a new shopping center opened in 2003, in the Galleria Colonna building. The church seen on the right is Santa Maria in Via, founded on the place where an image of the Virgin painted on a tile fell into the well; when the well overflowed, the image of the Virgin appeared to those nearby. Many pilgrims still come to drink the water of the famous well and to venerate the Madonna del Pozzo (Madonna of the Well).

This picture was taken in 1874 when the Central Station Termini had just been completed—the clock in the middle of the triangular facade had not yet been added. Construction began under Pope Pius IX when the railway first arrived in Rome, and it was completed in 1874 under Vittorio Emanuele II, the Savoy king after the unification of Italy. The station sits uncomfortably close to the Thermae, the baths that the emperor Diocletian built in the third century and whose ruins would have been visible on the far side of the piazza. On the left of the main entrance is a surviving corner of the Servian Wall, the most ancient wall of Rome.

A crossroads of people and cultures, the station was demolished in 1938 under a scheme organized by Angelo Mazzoni. During the years of Fascist rule, the trains always had to run on time, by the order of Mussolini. The new station was completed only after World War II, in 1950. Seen from the outside, the structure has a cement shell with a sinuous, undulating movement that deserved the nickname of "Dinosaur." For the year 2000, the station was restyled and a shopping center with 140 retail outlets was added. The square in front is now called Piazza dei Cinquecento in memory of the 500 soldiers killed in Ethiopia in a military campaign in 1887, where Italy was defeated.

For a long time on the outskirts of Rome, the basilica of St. Maria Maggiore is the greatest of all Rome's churches dedicated to the Virgin Mary. It was founded in 432 after the Council of Ephesus proclaimed Mary the mother of God. The legend portrayed in the twelfth-century mosaic installed on the upper floor of the eighteenth-century loggia says that Mary appeared to a wealthy Christian and to Pope Liberius, directing them to build a church on the Esquiline Hill in the exact spot of a miraculous snowfall between August 4 and 5. For a long time the porch was the favorite place to burn heretical books. Its medieval bell tower is the tallest in Rome.

Every August 5, in a chapel inside the basilica, petals of white flowers are thrown to celebrate the miraculous snowfall. Inside, one can still find the most important Christian mosaics on the side of the central nave and the triumphal arch, along with the first gold brought back from the Americas by Christopher Columbus, which now adorns the ceiling. On the side of the main altar is the tomb of Gian Lorenzo Bernini, the greatest of Baroque artists. The column in front of the basilica is a noted relic; it is the only surviving example of a series of columns built to adorn the ancient basilica of Maxentius in the Roman Forum.

This piazza is to the rear of St. Maria Maggiore and faces the apse of the church created by the Baroque artist Carlo Rainaldi. The job fell to Rainaldi after the project put forward by Bernini was deemed too expensive. In the center stands the Egyptian obelisk moved here from the Mausoleum of Augustus. The picture includes a very interesting and rare view of the Villa Montaldo Peretti, whose gate is at the bottom left of the photo. The villa occupied most of the Esquiline and Viminal hills, and was built in 1585 by Pope Sixtus V, who was known for his relocation of obelisks from circuses and archaeological sites to the main squares of Rome.

The Renaissance Villa Montaldo Peretti was demolished at the end of the nineteenth century to make way for the first railway station and its network of roads. The level of the street was lowered by thirteen feet and the old palazzos demolished, including the house of Bernini. For 2000, the Piazza dell'Esquilino became partly pedestrianized and is now lit at night. Nearby is the Theater of Opera, ranked among Italy's finest, which stages performances indoors in the winter, and in the summer moves to open-air venues around the city, including the historic Baths of Caracalla.

After 1870, a piazza was created in the shape of a semicircle, following the form of an ancient *exedra*, a building that housed a continuous bench used in ancient Rome and Greece for holding lectures. This was part of the ancient baths built by Diocletian in 298 using the labor of 40,000 slaves. Here Romans could exercise and play ball games in front of the Calidarium, a pool of hot water. In 1888, when this picture was taken, Alessandro Guerrieri created a fountain in the middle of the new piazza and decorated it with images of Egyptian lions. In the background, to the left, is the old Termini Station and the Palazzo Massimo.

In 1900 the fountain was replaced with another by Mario Rutelli, who decorated it with sensual, naked naiads (nymphs of the sea). The explicit nature of the statue caused such a sensation that, when it was completed, the surrounding high fence wasn't removed, for decency's sake. Finally, some youngsters removed the fence during the night, and the day after the city admired Rutelli's vision. The fences were left down, although no official inauguration of the fountain was held. The building in the background, partly hidden by trees, is the Palazzo Massimo, which now hosts the most important museum of ancient art in Rome, the Museo Nazionale Romano.

The palace stands on the top of the highest hill in Rome, the Quirinal Hill. Considered from ancient times to be a healthy place to live, it consequently attracted the most wealthy families of Rome. In Renaissance times the popes decided to build a palace here as a summer residence. This house was so beloved by the papacy that sometimes it was used as their main residence. For this reason the palace was embellished with masterpieces by Renaissance and Baroque artists. The granite fountain in front comes from the Roman Forum and the obelisk on top was taken from the Mausoleum of Octavian Augustus. The two figures on either side of the fountain are Castor and Pollux, transferred here from the nearby ruins of the Baths of Constantine.

The palace is now the residence of the president of Italy and this is why, along with the Italian flag on top of the building, the personal flag of the president is displayed when he is in Rome. Inside the palace are beautiful gardens that are opened to the public once a year on June 2, the anniversary of the republic. The palace itself is open to visitors every Sunday morning. The palace also houses the biggest carpet in Europe in the Hall of the Feasts, while the nearby Scuderie del Quirinale, the ancient stables of the palace, are used to host art exhibitions. Outside, the *corazzieri* (special guards of the president) watch over the palace. Each member of the corps must stand at least six feet tall.

Above: Named after the column erected for the victories of the emperor Marcus Aurelius against the Germans and Sarmatians in 180 (portrayed in the opening scenes of the movie *Gladiator*), this was the liveliest square in the city and was considered to be the social center of Rome. It was a piazza with an abundance of cafés and, for a long time, was the only place where coffee was roasted. There were also lemonade kiosks, watermelon sellers, porters waiting for jobs, and concerts in the open air. The statue of the emperor on top of the 137-foot column was replaced with a statue of St. Paul in 1587, which was more in style with the Catholic tastes of the city.

Right: Today the piazza is the heart of the Italian government, which has offices in the sixteenth-century Palazzo Chigi, the building at the right of the picture. The Palazzo Chigi houses the prime minister and further along, on the same side, the parliament is housed in the Palazzo Montecitorio. Nowadays, demonstrations against the government are held here. The square is largely a pedestrian area that, in the wake of terrorist threats, is carefully monitored by police. In the background of the picture is the main office of the *Il Tempo* newspaper, which is ideally located to cover both government business and protests against the government.

This picture was taken in 1944 and depicts a military parade of the Allies, following the city's liberation in June of the same year. The site has an important political resonance: the Piazza Venezia is located next to the Palazzo Venezia, which housed the headquarters of Mussolini for fourteen years. During his time in power it was a restricted area, with police constantly stopping people and asking for identification. In the background is the Vittoriano, the monument in memory of Vittorio Emanuele II, first king of Italy, created after his death. It was started in 1885 but was not opened until 1911. During the Fascist regime, Mussolini held military parades on the piazza, which led Romans to call it the "Piano"—the whiteness of the marble steps contrasted with the Fascists, dressed in black, looking like the keys of a piano.

Today there are military parades every June 2 to celebrate the republic, held along Via dei Fori Imperiali and in the Vittoriano, which is said to house the altar of the nation. The Vittoriano is now known as the "Wedding Cake" for its huge, white appearance. Following refurbishment, it has reopened to the public and, like Pincio Hill, offers a great view of Rome. The statue of the king is very big, a forty-foot bronze equestrian statue. The structure supporting it housed a dinner for twenty-one on its opening in 1911. In the Vittoriano are three museums covering the history of the monument and the history of the unification of Italy. There is also a modern art space for temporary exhibitions. The Vittoriano was closed for some days after eighteen Italians, including twelve members of the Carabinieri (the Italian special forces), were killed in Nasiriya, Iraq, in 2003. The monument was filled with flowers.

Until the nineteenth century, the piazza was much smaller, going under the name of Piazza St. Marco. In place of the Vittoriano was the Palazzetto Venezia (left), which abutted the Palazzo Venezia (right), and the Palazzo Torlonia (not shown), which faced the Palazzo Venezia on the opposite side of the square. It was the finish for horse races held during the Roman Carnival. The Palazzo Venezia was built by a Venetian cardinal, Pietro Barbo, who became Pope Paul II. It was used as a summer residence of the popes until the Quirinal Palace was built, then was given to the republic of Venice. From the Venetians it passed to the Austrian monarchy, and then Mussolini set up his headquarters on the first floor. The balcony in the center of the facade of Palazzo Venezia was used by Mussolini for his speeches to the people. The dictator would keep his office light on at night to show that he was working.

While the work on the Vittoriano was in progress from 1885 to 1911, there were many changes to the square. The Palazzetto Venezia was moved to the far end of the Piazzetta St. Marco; the Palazzo Torlonia was replaced with a copy of the Palazzo Venezia, the so-called Palazzo delle Assicurazioni Generali; and the house of Michelangelo was demolished. The *fasci littori* (symbols of Fascism) on the facade were removed after the fall of Mussolini and liberation of Italy by the Allies. The palazzo is now used for art exhibitions. It also houses the National Museum of Decorative Arts and one of the most specialized libraries of art and archaeology in Rome. It is at a crossroads that links the modern downtown area to ancient Rome.

The equestrian statue of Marcus Aurelius stands impressively in the middle of the Capitoline Square, located on the smallest hill in Rome. The Capitoline Hill is the location for important religious and political ceremonies, most often held between the Palazzo Nuovo and Palazzo dei Conservatori. The statue has been standing since the 1500s, when the Piazza del Campidoglio was restyled by Michelangelo. It is a very rare bronze statue, saved from being melted down and recast only because it was believed to represent the Christian emperor Constantine. In reality, this is a pagan emperor, Marcus Aurelius, who has been elevated in the midst of the most Catholic city for centuries, gazing toward the Vatican. Since the Middle Ages the Capitoline Hill has also been called Monte Caprino (Mount of the Goats).

The small boys are gone and the posts are different, but little else has changed. This statue is a copy of the original and was finally erected in 1997 after twenty years of planning and preparation. The original is now preserved in the courtyard of the Capitoline Museum, just to the side of the piazza. The statue, like the she-wolf, is increasingly recognized as a symbol of Rome. Its depiction on the fifty-cent coin, after the euro was introduced to replace the lira, has reinforced this view. The palace behind the statue houses the city hall. It has two completely different sides: this one is of the Renaissance, and the opposite side, facing the Roman Forum, is ancient. Everywhere is the emblem of Rome, SPQR: *Senatus Populus que Romanus* (the Senate and People of Rome). The emblem, representing the city hall, can be seen on lampposts, trash cans, and buses.

This small piazza with cafés and restaurants lies at the foot of the Cordonata, the stairway with wide and low steps created by Michelangelo so that horses could reach the Piazza del Campidoglio. The square was bordered on the right by a street leading to the Theater of Marcello and the Cattle Market and on the left by a street leading to the former Piazza St. Marco, now renamed Piazza Venezia. Only a part of the other stairway leading to the Church of St. Maria in Aracoeli can be seen. A market was held in this piazza until it was moved to the Piazza Navona and then to Campo dei Fiori. Since then, a lot of *burini* (people from the countryside) seeking jobs in the city would sleep on the stairway during the night.

The big apartment building on the left, as well as the convent and beautiful cloister of the Church of St. Maria in Aracoeli, were demolished to create the Vittoriano, visible at the top left of the picture. During the building of the Vittoriano, at the foot of the stairway of the Church of St. Maria, an *insula* (ancient residence) and the small medieval Church of St. Biagio in Mercatello were found. The sixteenth-century fountain survived, as well as the facade of the Campidoglio and the Church of St. Maria in Aracoeli. Inside the church, a wonderful old statue of the baby Jesus (every baby born in Rome was said to be as beautiful as the baby of Aracoeli) was stolen a few years ago and has yet to be recovered. The bell of the Capitoline Tower was also stolen and can no longer ring out to announce the death of the pope.

Left: To one side of the Capitoline Hill can be found the infamous Tarpeian Hill. This was the place where disabled children, criminals, and betrayers of the nation were pushed down from the hill and killed. The place takes the name from the first betrayer of Rome, a woman who opened the Capitoline walls to the marauding Sabines. She was reputedly smashed to a pulp by their shields because they too did not like traitors. The church on the right is St. Maria della Consolazione, annexed to the Hospital of Consolation and famous for the burning of prohibited books during Easter time. Mothers who had sons in jail waiting to be executed prayed to the image of the Madonna preserved in the church to spare them. Nearby, the Church of St. Giovanni Decollato (St. John the Beheaded) disposed of the bodies of executed criminals who didn't have the money to be buried.

Right: The area around the Tarpeian Hill was cleared by Mussolini to give Romans a glimpse of their violent past. A number of historical buildings on the left were demolished, along with the Hospital of Consolation. On the right is a narrow street leading to the Church of St. Giorgio al Velabro and other characteristic *vicoli* (narrow streets) saved from Mussolini's wrecking ball. Of special interest is the change in the street level between old and new—this phenomenon of lowering the street level is one that occurs in many places across Rome.

This was the heart of the political, commercial, and religious life of Rome from 600 BC, during the monarchy, and through to the times of the republic and the empire. The Roman Forum was filled up with silt brought in by the flooding river Tiber during the Middle Ages, which ultimately helped preserve it. Further up the hill, the building with the bell tower shows the stratification of building styles on one site. At the base the style is ancient; this was the site of the archives of the Roman Empire, the Tabularium, where the trial of Jesus was held. A tower was added to the city hall by Pope Nicholas V in the fifteenth century and was used as an observatory for the astronomers at the university. On the right, behind the Arch of Septimius Severus, is the Convent of St. Maria in Aracoeli; on the left, through the three columns of the Temple of Castor and Pollux, is the area built on the Tarpeian Hill.

Excavations at the Forum have been going on since the unification of Italy, accelerated during the time of Mussolini. "Il Duce" wanted to be celebrated as a new emperor, so he made great efforts to enhance the Roman Forum, the political center and symbol of the Roman Empire. The Arch of Septimius Severus, conqueror of Parthia (modern-day Iran), has been further revealed and the Convent of St. Maria in Aracoeli was destroyed to make room for the Vittoriano. On the other side of this photograph, behind the three columns of the Temple of Castor and Pollux, a housing quarter has been demolished, revealing the Tarpeian Hill. It is amazing to see the number of pieces of decorated marble on the side of the street by the Roman Forum. These historic relics used to be snatched by tourists eager to return home with a Roman souvenir.

Few could imagine today that the glorious center of ancient Rome had become known as the Campo Vaccino (Cattle Field), a pasture for the many cows, sheep, and goats kept in the heart of the city. The glorious Roman Forum, the monumental square that was the center of the great Roman Empire and the stage of many triumphal processions, had been filled by the silt from the floods of the Tiber, which had covered most of the original buildings. This was originally the Temple of Antoninus and Faustine, transformed into the Church of St. Lorenzo in Miranda during the seventeenth century. The best-preserved parts of the temple are the columns and the architrave, dedicated to "Divo Antonino et Diva Faustina," a deified emperor and empress from the second century. Emperors could be deified if they were believed to have been seen flying to heaven on the top of an eagle. What actually happened was that, when an emperor died, an eagle was released into the sky while someone proclaimed that they had seen the emperor on top of the eagle.

During the time of Mussolini, in the demagogic era of the "New Empire" declared by the Fascist dictator in 1934, the Roman Forum began to be excavated and the ancient level of Rome started to appear once more. The excavations revealed the original level of the Roman Forum, which was in some places up to twenty-two feet below the medieval cattle field. Because of subsequent excavations, the door of the church is now too high to be used as the main entrance, which is now found at the back of the church.

INSIGNE·RELIGIONIS·ATQVE·ARTIS·MONVMENTVM
VETVSTATE·FATISCENS
PIVS·SEPTIMVS·PONTIFEX·MAX
NOVIS·OPERIBVS·PRISCVM·EXEMPLAR·IMITANTIBVS
FVLCIRI·SERVARIQVE·IVSSIT
ANNO·SACRI·PRINCIPATVS·EIVS·XXIIII

The Triumphal Arch of Titus celebrates the victory of the emperors Vespasian and Titus in Jerusalem in AD 70. In the panels inside the arch are found bas-reliefs representing the triumphal procession, which took place on the sacred way, Via Sacra, passing through the arch. They show the spoils of war pillaged from the Temple of Jerusalem, destroyed during that campaign by the Romans. The arch was actually called the Arch of the Seven Lucerne during the Middle Ages and was transformed into the fortress of the Frangipane family, which was cleared in 1821—the ruins can still be seen on the right.

The walls of the fortress no longer stand, and the street has been covered by the big cobblestones in the style used by the Romans to build streets in ancient times. The dedication on the top is modern and recalls a restoration of the arch committed by Pope Pius VII in the nineteenth century. What really happened to the spoils of that war still remains the subject of dispute. Legend says that the sacred menorah (a seven-branched candelabra) lies underneath the Broken Bridge, or that it was removed when the Goths sacked Rome. To this day, many Orthodox Jews refuse to walk through the arch because of its connection to Titus's destruction of Jerusalem.

The three barrel vaults (shown here in 1865) belong to the side nave of the basilica, started in 306 by the emperor Maxentius and finished by his successor, Constantine. It had huge proportions: it was 260 feet long, 200 feet wide, and eighty feet high. The central nave, with the colossal statue of Constantine and a side nave, collapsed in the Middle Ages and the marble decorating the structure was reused for St. Peter's Basilica in the sixteenth century. Although the term "basilica" is now used to describe churches, in ancient times basilicas housed indoor markets, houses of justice, and auditoriums. Early Christians copied the shape of these structures to build houses of worship; this is why the word is now used to define churches.

Little has changed to the main structure, and this basilica is still the most prominent monument in Rome when viewed from any high point in the city. The grand Renaissance entrance, which can be seen opposite the barrel vaults in the earlier view, has been moved to Via di St. Gregorio on the Palatine Hill. The Basilica of Maxentius has been an important inspiration for a variety of artists, including Michelangelo when he built the new St. Peter's in the sixteenth century.

To the left is the Arch of Constantine (seen from the side) and in front of it is the ancient Meta Sudans fountain, around which the chariot racers used to turn in the circuses. In the background of this 1870 picture are the ruins of the apse of the Temple of Venus and Rome, planned and opened by Emperor Adrian in AD 135. Legend says that the architect Apollodorus, the official architect of the previous emperor, Trajan, was harsh in his criticism of the shape of the temple. Not one to take criticism lightly, Emperor Adrian chopped his head off.

Today the area is restricted by fences and the Temple of Venus and Rome can only be viewed from afar. The Meta Sudans, the only ancient fountain to survive to the modern era, was destroyed by Mussolini when he constructed the Via dei Fori Imperiali. The Roman Forum in the background and the Palatine Hill on the left are surrounded by fences restricting visitors' access during the daytime. The Palatine is the cradle of Rome, where Romulus and Remus founded the city and the emperors had their palaces.

The arch celebrates the victory of the emperor Constantine over his rival, Maxentius, in 312. Legend has it that before the battle, a cross appeared to Constantine and the voice of God told him, "With this sign you will win." So Constantine decorated the shields and beams of his army with crosses, attacked Maxentius, and won—helped by the cross. There are no crosses visible on the arch, most probably because the legend was founded later, when Rome became a Christian city. One can see this legend represented in the rooms painted by Raphael in the Vatican museums. Constantine legalized Christianity in 313 and from that time the persecutions against Christians stopped. The cone-shaped Meta Sudans fountain is to the right.

The biggest difference between the two photos, apart from the fences, is the disappearance of the Meta Sudans, which was demolished by Mussolini to make way for the Via dei Fori Imperiali. He used it for Fascist military parades to connect the Piazza Venezia, where he had his headquarters, with the Colosseum, the symbol of the power of the Roman Empire. The Arch of Constantine is still in excellent condition and has escaped the fate of many other old Roman structures, which were destroyed and their marble recycled to build new churches. This is because everything linked to the memory of Constantine, the first Christian emperor, is celebrated, honored, and considered sacred. In the background is Via di San Gregorio, which runs between the Colosseum and the Circus Maximus.

The Colosseum used to stand at the edge of the city. The eighty entrances, half-buried by the silt of the floods, have no fences. This famous building was completed in just eight years by the emperor Vespasian of the Flavian dynasty, to offer *panem et circenses* (free bread and games) to the citizens of Rome. It was used for gladiator fights, the hunting of wild animals, and was sometimes flooded to reenact sea battles. A great many slaves, most of whom were taken to Rome after the repression of the civil wars in Judea in AD 70, were employed in the construction of the Colosseum. The gladiator fights continued until 405, and hunting until the sixth century, after which the Colosseum was robbed of its stonework. The 300 tons of iron used for clamping the stone was removed in the Middle Ages, creating holes in the structure. However, this was not nearly as drastic as some of the ideas of the popes, who wished to destroy the structure or use it for industrial purposes.

According to prophecy, "As long as the Colosseum stands, Rome will stand; when the Colosseum falls, Rome will fall." In the 1990s a restoration program took place, with the white limestone cleaned of the dirt caused by pollution. The Via dei Fori Imperiali was closed to traffic on Sundays to reduce vibrations and pollution. Today the Colosseum is used for special events: the pope ends the "Stations of the Cross" Easter service inside the structure, and there are also occasional concerts, including a recent one by Paul McCartney. The area is full of costumed gladiators posing with tourists for pictures. It is also filled with cats that are fed by the local residents, who are particularly fond of these animals. Ancient mosaics portraying the games that were once held inside the Colosseum can be found in the Borghese Gallery.

This photo, taken around 1865, shows the inside of the amphitheater filled by silt and a great number of altars installed around the arena floor for the "Stations of the Cross" service. They were built in 1756 by Pope Benedictus XIV, who consecrated the monument to the Passion of Jesus, thus preventing any further reduction of the building. According to some traditional accounts, a lot of Christians were killed by wild beasts in the arena during the persecutions, although there is little documentary evidence to support this claim. The marble used in the four levels of the *cavea* (sitting area) has long since been removed to construct churches in places such as the Palazzo della Cancelleria, Palazzo Venezia, Palazzo Barberini, and Palazzo Farnese, as well as St. Peter's Basilica.

The altars around the stage were demolished in 1873 and the storerooms underneath the arena were excavated at the end of the twentieth century, revealing trapdoors, animal cages, elevators, and rooms for the storage of the gladiators' weapons. A small part of the sitting area was rebuilt by Mussolini to show the division in social classes inside of the structure: the first level was for the rich patrician classes, the second for the knights, the third for the "plebs," and the fourth for poor women. The building could house up to 70,000 people. Today it is visited by three million people a year.

The Columns of Nerva rest on the porch of the Temple of Minerva, the Roman equivalent of the Greek goddess Athena. In the nineteenth century the building was used as a *forno* (bakery). The Temple of Minerva was in the Foro di Nerva, or Transitorio, an ancient monumental square created by the emperor Nerva in AD 97 to link the popular Suburra area—where Julius Caesar was born—to the Roman Forum. During the Middle Ages the columns were also called the Arca di Noé (Noah Arch) by the corruption of the words "architrave of Nerva."

The street of the empire, Via dei Fori Imperiali, built by Mussolini in the 1930s, only served to separate the monumental squares added by the emperors on the side of the ancient Roman Forum. Excavation has revealed the ancient levels, the bakery has been removed, and the columns further exposed. They can now be viewed from the higher street level. This difference of levels is not only due to silt being brought in by the repeated flooding of the Tiber, which ceased with its flood-protection measures in 1988, but because many new buildings have been constructed on top of the ancient ones—60 percent of ancient Rome still lies beneath modern Rome. This is one of the reasons why the subway system is so underdeveloped.

This was a familiar site for those taking a grand tour of Europe at the end of the nineteenth century, when sheep, goats, and cows often wandered around the ancient ruins found in the inhabited city. Not far from the Column of Trajan, seen here in the background, was the Capitoline Hill—in former days called the "Mount of the Goats." It was once a familiar practice for herdsmen to come into the city each morning and wait at the main crossroads and squares to collect fresh milk directly from the goats.

The area around the column has been excavated to recover the ancient square where it was erected. The Column of Trajan, carved in the shape of rolled papyrus, has a height of ninety-seven feet and it represents the successful military campaign of the emperor Trajan against Dacia (modern-day Romania) in AD 106. He pillaged so many treasures that he could afford the building of this new monumental square, considered one of the wonders of Rome. Where now there are two churches he built two libraries, one housing books written in Greek and one housing books written in Latin. The Vatican replaced the statue of Trajan on the top of the column with a statue of St. Peter, made from the recast bronze of five church doors, a cannon from Castle St. Angelo, and a decoration from the Pantheon. In 2000, a new excavation program was started to recover other monumental squares.

This market, built around AD 107, was designed by the architect Apollodoro di Damasco, the favorite of Emperor Trajan. Though he was killed by Trajan's successor, Adrian, the market survived. When this picture was taken in 1911, remnants of the markets were barely visible, occupied as they were by orchards and stores. Until the nineteenth century, tourists had to ask a baker if they wanted to visit the ancient site, which lay within the Alessandrino quarter, built in 1570 on the monumental squares of the emperors Augustus, Nerva, Julius Caesar, and Vespasian. It was named after the man who built it: Cardinal Bonelli, who was also known as Alessandrino because he was born in the city of Alexandria, in northern Egypt.

Cleared during the 1930s, the markets are now a national monument and a popular sight for visitors to Rome. The site of the ancient markets—which occupied six levels—was cut into the Quirinal Hill and divided in two by a street called Via Biberatica, from either the word *bibere*, which in Latin means "drink," or from *piperatica*, meaning "pepper," possibly from the spice storerooms located in the area. In the Middle Ages the market buildings were partly transformed into a convent. The tower was part of the fortress also built on the markets and belonging to the Caetani family. According to legend, the emperor Nero fiddled from the top of this tower while Rome burned in AD 64. However, this would have been difficult even for a man of Nero's imagination, as the tower was not built until the twelfth century.

A botanical garden was established here on the Palatine Hill in the ruins of the palaces of the emperors. It was from here that the emperors gave the starting signal to the chariot races held in the Circus Maximus. At the foot of the hill, at number 43 on Via dei Cerchi, an ancient marble hand with the forefinger raised, called the "Hand of Cicerone," was used in the Middle Ages to show the price of wine, one *bajocco* (coin) per *fojetta* (half a liter). In the same street there were public executions: the last one to occur here was in 1861, while the last in Rome was in 1868 in the Piazza del Popolo.

Now the Palatine Hill is an archaeological site open to public, with a museum documenting the history of the hill, from the foundation of the *poemerium*, the ancient sacred area where Rome was founded, to the decorations found in the palaces, such as a relief with the most ancient testimonies of Roman history. Unfortunately, the most ancient part of the Palatine Hill, where the hut of Romulus was discovered, is closed to the public but can be visited on request.

The Circus Maximus was the biggest chariot-racing track in Rome, holding over 300,000 people at the kind of races depicted in the 1959 film *Ben Hur*. It was 656 yards long and 218 yards wide. The practice of chariot racing had begun before the Roman republic, under the king Tarquino Prisco. During the reign of the emperors, several obelisks were moved to the center of the track from Egypt. These can now be found in the Piazza del Popolo and St. John in Lateran. After the fall of the Roman Empire, the area was gradually stripped of its building materials and turned into a marketplace with large sheds; it was later used as a dormitory for poor people when the market was moved to Via Manzoni.

The dormitory buildings were cleared in 1934 and the space is now used on occasion for parades, demonstrations, and celebrations such as a championship victory for one of the big Roman soccer teams, Roma or Lazio. All that is left of the circus is the oval shape, now filled by meadows and slopes in place of the seating area. The last chariot event is believed to have taken place in 549 under the king of the invading Goths, Totila. These days Italians have transferred their affection for wheel-to-wheel action to Formula 1 car racing and their beloved Ferraris.

This medieval well was built on the site of the *frigidarium*, the open area of the Baths of Caracalla that contained a cold-water bath. Built in 212 with a capacity of around 2,000, the baths were in use until 537, when the Goths cut the flow of water from the aqueducts that fed them. The ancient baths offered free facilities where people could relax and keep fit.

In the Middle Ages the baths were used as a cemetery and then as a refuge for the poor. Most of the original decorations are now installed in the churches, palaces, and squares of Rome. Some statues, once preserved in the collection of the Farnese family, were moved to Naples. Shelley's poem *Prometheus Unbound* was written in the ruins of these baths.

The medieval well was replaced with a simple grating, visible in the foreground. Nowadays the baths are a much-visited place, and they host operas and concerts during the summer, a tradition started by Mussolini. The dictator would make an appearance in his Alfa Romeo during the summer events, driving to the baths through a tunnel linking his headquarters, Palazzo Venezia, with the venue.

When a pope is elected, he has to come and take possession of the Cathedral of St. Giovanni in Laterano. Few realize that this is the "mother church of Rome and the world," the first church founded by Constantine, and still the city's cathedral. Gentile de Fabriano, an Italian painter of frescoes and altarpieces in the Gothic style, was working on a series of frescoes for the church when he died. Sadly, the frescoes, finished by Pisanello, were later destroyed. The blessing of the cathedral was a much-photographed happening, even in the early days of photography; this picture dates to 1868. The awning for the blessing was used as protection from the sun and rain but also as a means of amplifying the voice of the pope. The last restyling of the building was completed in the eighteenth century, although the magnificent central bronze door comes from the Senate House in the Forum.

The orange building seen on the right is the Lateran Museum and the Curia, which houses various offices of the Vatican, including the Vatican court for the annulment of marriages. Here the Lateran Treaty between Mussolini and the pope was signed on February 11, 1929. On the right, hidden by trees, is the famous Scala Santa, the legendary staircase from Pontius Pilate's palace in Jerusalem, descended by Christ and now ascended by pilgrims on their knees. On the left are the Aurelian Walls with the Porta San Giovanni and the Porta Asinaria, two of Rome's best-preserved ancient gates, leading to a huge clothes market that takes place every morning on Via Sannio. To this day the old tradition continues, as the pope still comes to St. Giovanni in Laterano to take possession of the cathedral when he is elected.

The square of Bocca della Verità, seen here in 1865, was used as a cattle market; it was the meeting place of the *burini* (from *bue*, "bull") people coming in from the countryside. Some burini are standing at the fountain of Tritons. As at other fountains in Rome, women used the surrounding stones to beat clothes to wash them. In the 1800s, this place was at the edge of the city and there were many haylofts in the surrounding buildings. The fountain was created by Bizzaccheri in 1715, taking inspiration from Bernini's fountain of Triton in the Piazza Barberini. The circular temple is that of Hercules, who was often called "Olivarius" because he was the protector of the olive-oil producers. It was transformed into a church dedicated to St. Mary del Sole in the twelfth century.

The building on the right of the original picture was demolished, along with other local businesses, and the area was cleared by Mussolini to create Via del Mare, a road to the Mediterranean. He was intent on creating a new development area for Rome in the 1940s, before World War II intervened. Today in the area there are "Mussolinian" buildings with offices of the city hall flanking Via del Mare, now called Via Petroselli, and Via del Teatro di Marcello, which runs toward the Piazza Venezia.

The Temple of Fortuna Virile was transformed in the tenth century into a church dedicated to St. Maria Egiziaca, shown here in 1890. The eighteenth-century church in the background is St. Maria in Cosmedin, with its Baroque facade. In the portico of the St. Maria church is the famous "Mouth of Truth," a drain cover with the face of a river god, used in the Middle Ages to test the truth in commercial transactions held in the marketplace. If a trader put his hand in after telling a lie, the river god bit it off. The story goes that once a woman was taken there to test her fidelity to her husband. During the trip to face the Mouth of Truth, her lover, acting like a madman, jumped into the cart and kissed her. So when she faced the river god she could truly say that only her husband and the insane man from the crowd had ever kissed her.

The surrounding quarter was yet another to be demolished by Mussolini to create a road to the sea. Fortunately, the temples were saved and this is now one of the best-preserved examples in Rome. The Church of St. Maria in Cosmedin was restored in 1894 and its facade was reconstructed in its original Romanesque form. Today a lot of tourists mimic Gregory Peck and Audrey Hepburn from the film *Roman Holiday* and line up to put their hands in the Mouth of Truth, following the ancient tradition.

This seventh-century church, once dedicated to St. Sebastian, who was killed here and then thrown in the sewers of Rome, was built on an important city site. The Velabro was a marshy place where the twin brothers Romulus and Remus were fed by a she-wolf and then found by the shepherd Faustolo. In the 1800s there was a *burdelletto*, a brothel for the stockmen and shepherds of the area. This spot, part of the ancient cattle market, the Foro Boario, was the center for money changers who had plenty of business in the shade of the arch just on the side of the church. The Arcus Argentarium (Arch of the Silversmiths) was built by the money changers in 204 in honor of the emperor Septimius Severus and his family. There was said to be treasure lodged somewhere in the arch, which is why there are many holes in the marble, drilled by people trying to find the treasure. On the left is a bigger arch, the Arch of Gianus, an ancient doorway to the cattle market.

A bomb explosion in 1993 destroyed the portico of the church, but
it has been carefully restored. It is now one of the most popular churches
for weddings, admired for its medieval shape untouched by the Baroque
era. The area around the two arches is now restricted by fences and is a
very quiet place. The ancient sewer of Rome, the Cloaca Maxima, which
has an access point in front of the church, can be visited by making
arrangements with the administrators at the city hall.

Begun by Julius Caesar and completed by his successor, Augustus, who named it after his nephew, the semicircular theater presented tragedies and comedies. For the tragedies, criminals replaced the main characters and were sometimes literally butchered on stage. Later, the theater was transformed into a fortress and then the upper levels were turned into a Renaissance palace, while the half-sunken arches on the lower levels were used as garages and stores. This picturesque street facing the arches was called Via dei Sugherari after the shops selling *sughero* (corks). It led to the Piazza Montanara, named after a family of that name, but the name was appropriate because it was the gathering place for people who came from the mountains surrounding Rome. This picture dates to 1880.

Mussolini separated the theater from its adjoining buildings between 1926 and 1929, during the creation of the road to the sea. All the traditional stores, narrow streets, and the Piazza Montanara were destroyed. In the process, workers found columns belonging to the Temple of Apollo Sosiano, reerected here in 1940, as well as some of the arcades of the Theater of Marcellus. These were re-created in brownstone to distinguish it from the original structure. In the summer, the theater presents classical concerts. Private apartments of rich families are still found inside the theater, a vestige of earlier times.

This 1880 view shows the main street of what became known as the Jewish ghetto. Through the arches of the ancient porch of Octavia is the *foro piscario* (fish market), which was held here from ancient times. The fish were laid out on the recycled marble banks on either side of the street. The cost of the fish was fixed by the *cottiatori* (auctioneers), which comes from the Latin word *cotidie* (daily). This was also the main entrance to the Jewish quarter established here by Pope Paul IV, the father of the Inquisition, in 1555. The ancient Jewish community, at the time numbering 5,000, was isolated in this tiny area of four apartment buildings. Although they were usually confined indoors, women would still try to visit the renowned Jewish fortune-tellers. Even though they were ostracized by Roman society, Jewish physicians were still acknowledged to be the best in their profession.

One of the first acts of the young Italian state in 1870 was to tear down the Jewish quarter's walls and demolish the apartment buildings on the left side of Via Portico d'Ottavia. New buildings were constructed and a synagogue was built here in 1904. Via Portico d'Ottavia is the main street of what is still known locally as the Jewish ghetto, with good restaurants offering traditional Jewish-Roman cuisine such as fried artichokes, fried codfish, and kosher dishes. At the end of the street, one of the best bakeries in Rome can be found.

In this picture, the Portico d'Ottavia is viewed from the west, showing its ancient, columned *propylaeum* (entrance). This porch was built by the emperor Octavian Augustus and named after his sister Octavia, the repudiated wife of Marcus Antonius. It was grand enough to include temples and libraries, and it acted as a foyer to entertain the people who were waiting to watch plays in the nearby Theater of Marcellus. In the Middle Ages the Portico d'Ottavia was partly transformed into the Church of St. Angelo in the *pescheria* (fish market area) alongside it. There is even a small chapel specifically set aside for the fish merchants. The dome in the background belongs to the Baroque church of St. Maria in Campitelli.

On October 16, 1943, in front of this porch more than 1,000 Jews were gathered to be deported to Auschwitz—they were told that if they gathered 110 pounds of gold they would avoid deportation. Only fifteen returned alive, and none of the 200 children returned.

The area in front of the porch was recently restored and reduced to the ancient level of the area on the side of the Theater of Marcellus; it was opened in 2003 with a meeting of the mayor of Rome and the chief rabbi of the Roman Jewish community.

Tiber Island, the only island on the river, always had the rough shape of a ship; in ancient times there was a temple built to the god of medicine, Aesculapius, in the shape of a ship. Remains of this temple can still be seen on the downstream side, saved by superstitious Romans. Until 1888, palaces were built on the edges of the riverbanks, which were always the first part of the city to be flooded. The island is connected on the right to the Jewish quarter, and this picture shows the buildings before the demolitions that occurred after the unification of Italy. The linking bridge is the second-oldest surviving bridge in Rome and was built by Fabricius in 62 BC. To the left is the Caestius Bridge, linking the island to Trastevere. The domes visible beyond the Jewish quarter belong to the churches of St. Carlo ai Catinari and St. Andrea della Valle.

On the right, beyond the trees grown on the Lungotevere, is the Assyrian Babylonian dome of the modern synagogue, visible from all over Rome. Built in 1904, it caters to a community of 10,000 and was visited in 1986 by Pope John Paul II, the first pope to offer such a gesture of conciliation. Inside is a museum of the Holocaust and some ancient works of art saved from earlier synagogues in the city. Tiber Island and the banks of the river now have protective embankments that prevent flooding. The island has maintained its connection to medicine, as it is still a center for hospitals. The broken bridge in the foreground, Ponte Rotto, has suffered so much damage since it was built in the second century BC—it was the first stone bridge to be built on the river—that in the end the city stopped repairing it.

Left: Established in 220, this church may well be the oldest dedicated to St. Maria. The church itself is from the twelfth century, while the porch was built in the sixteenth century—on the top of the facade there is a fascinating medieval mosaic. Inside, the columns dividing the church into three naves are from the Baths of Caracalla. When the *bulli* (proud, bold, and arrogant Roman youths) graduated from their adventurous lives, they traditionally left their knives here.

Above: The piazza, in the heart of the Trastevere district, has maintained its medieval appearance. The people living in this quarter are proud to be Trasteverini, claiming to be the only real Romans left. Although the area is fairly popular with tourists today, there are still many artisan stores and traditional Roman restaurants and pubs. In July there is a special feast in this area, the Festa de Noantri, with markets and music to celebrate the local pride of being a Trasteverini.

This is one of the three gates in the Aurelian Wall on the other side of the river, protecting Trastevere. It was repaired by the corrupt pope Alexander VI, who reigned from 1492 to 1503, and reinforced with *merlones* (battlements)—seven are visible above the parapet shown in this photograph from 1870. The name of the gate comes from either the emperor Septimius Severus or the gardens of his son, Settimio Geta. Tradition claims that the building to the right was the house of La Fornarina, a local baker whose daughter was supposed to be the lover of Raphael. This spot shows the proletarian appearance of the district, which was the home of many seafarers. To the left of the gate is a fresco depicting Jesus.

This is another Roman quarter loved by visitors because of its medieval appearance. Today almost every corner of this place has beautiful cafés and in the house of La Fornarina there is now a restaurant. On the right side of the gate is the American John Cabot University and the Villa Farnesina (with Raphael's frescoes); on the left is the Botanical Gardens, another place for taking a leisurely stroll. The street on the left, now called Via Garibaldi, leads to the Gianicolo Hill.

Left: Although the Gianicolo Hill was not located within the city walls, it has always been used as a Roman defense, mainly during the unification of Italy. Garibaldi tried to start the unification with an assault on Rome from the Gianicolo Hill by fighting against French soldiers protecting the pope. After a terrible campaign in 1848–49, he decided to give up and start again from the south. It would be another twenty-one years before his objective was achieved. This statue, which was unveiled in 1895, shows Garibaldi gazing toward the Vatican, or, maybe more romantically, toward his courageous wife, Anita, whose statue and tomb lie further down the hill. The tomb of Garibaldi himself is in Sardinia, on the island of Caprera, where he died.

Right: Though the monument is no longer surrounded by cultivated fields, the area has managed to preserve its parks, and it is still worth climbing the hill for its spectacular views over Rome and the Tempietto of Bramante, the most characteristic work of the Renaissance. On the piazza there is a traditional puppet show, one of the few still surviving in Rome. This part of Rome is home to the American Academy and the United States embassy, which stands close to the beautiful parks of Villa Doria Pamphili and Villa Sciarra.

There is a remarkable view from the lighthouse on the Gianicolo Hill. Designed by Manfredo Manfredi, the lighthouse was given to the city of Rome by expatriate Italians from Argentina during the International Exposition of 1911. It was a curious sight during the night because it lit the area with the colors of the Italian flag. At the foot of the hill is the Regina Coeli prison where, in World War II, Jewish and political prisoners were kept before deportation to camps, and where 335 people were taken and killed in the Fosse Ardeatine as a retaliation for a guerrilla bomb that killed thirty-two German soldiers.

The lighthouse is still in operation. From this vantage point there is still a fine view over the whole city of Rome. To the left is Castel St. Angelo, surmounted by its angel, and the white mass of the Law Courts, nicknamed the "Palazzaccio" (Ugly Palace). Across the river is the Church of St. John of Florentines, and in the background the villa with two towers is the beautiful Villa Medici, designed by Raphael. At the foot of the hill, the Regina Coeli jail still stands.

The name of this portion of the river is the "Great Bank" because it was here that the biggest ships docked in the ports of Rome. It had been a port since ancient times, and until the end of 1800, Sicilian sailing ships could be seen anchored here, bringing the Romans' favorite Marsala wine. The water mills used to be a characteristic sight here, used since the siege of the Goths in 537 when they cut the aqueducts. They were usually built on the top of two flatboats anchored with big chains. The long building in the background of this picture, taken in 1887, is the Institute St. Michael, built in 1689 for orphans and abandoned children who were brought there to learn a trade.

The port was demolished in 1888 when the city planners built embankments on the side of the Tiber to prevent floods; the mills, however, were all destroyed in the terrible flood of 1870. The Institute St. Michael was transformed by Mussolini into a juvenile jail and a foundry. In World War II it was used first by the Germans, then by the Allies, and then by evacuees. It now houses the Ministry of Arts and the Instituto Centrale del Restauro, which is dedicated to the restoration of art.

There are three gates in the Aurelian Wall as it passes through the Trastevere district: Porta Portese, Porta Aurelia, and Porta Settimiana. Porta Portese, shown here in 1915, was restyled in the Baroque style in the seventeenth century by Pope Urban VIII and completed by Pope Innocent X. The gate is named after the road that begins here, the Portuense. It leads to Porto, the ancient port of Rome, which has now been transformed into the small town of Fiumicino. In the background, on the other side of the wall, are the buildings of the new customhouse.

The customhouse was demolished to build the Sublicio Bridge on the river, and at the same time, two extra openings were created in the wall for traffic. Since the end of World War II, there has been a well-attended flea market here every Sunday morning, stretching out a mile and a half toward Trastevere. By 10:00 a.m. it gets very crowded, so the best business is done early. Today the market is swamped with car parts, cassettes, and radios, but with luck and patience one can still find old furniture or bric-a-brac over which to barter.

Porta Ostiense was one of the oldest and best-preserved gates on the Aurelian Wall, renamed Porta San Paolo long after St. Paul walked through it on the way to his execution. To the left is the pyramid that was built in 330 days by the wealthy tribune of the people, Caio Cestio, who became interested in Egyptian culture after the conquest of Egypt. The pyramid was built before the creation of the Aurelian Wall in AD 271–275, so it was annexed into the structure. The area was close to the old port and there were a lot of marble artisans and wine warehouses in the Testaccio area, which explains the carts carrying wine in this picture. In the last few centuries, Romans would meet outside the Aurelian Wall in October to dance the *saltarello* and eat and drink at the surrounding restaurants.

The Aurelian Wall was partly destroyed during the occupation of the city by the anti-Nazi partisans in 1938. Today it is a very important connecting junction for buses and subways, and a busy district for nightlife. On the side of the pyramid is a Protestant cemetery with the tombs of the poets Keats and Shelley. Shelley's ashes were brought to the cemetery at Mary Shelley's request and were finally interred, after much obstruction, by the papal authorities. Keats lies next to his friend Joseph Severn in an old part of the cemetery near the pyramid of Caius Cestius, who died in 12 BC. Keats's gravestone bears the inscription, "Here lies One Whose Name was writ in Water."

Condemned for being a Christian, as a Roman citizen St. Paul had the "privilege" of being beheaded instead of crucified. His body was buried here, and in the fifth century a basilica was built over it. Partly destroyed by the Normans in 1084, the basilica was badly damaged in 1823 by a fire caused by two roofers spilling a bucket of hot coals. This 1865 picture shows the reconstructed basilica, the second-largest in Rome after St. Peter's, without the colonnade. The basilica still contains beautiful works of art that were saved from the fire, such as the original bronze door and the Passover candlestick.

In front of the basilica a *quadriportico* (courtyard) was added between 1890 and 1892. The columns are from Lake Maggiore, and it took four years to transport them to Rome. The statue of St. Paul was carved in one piece of Carrara marble weighing 400 tons and portrays a very severe Paul. The mosaic on the facade dates from 1854, but inside is an original from the thirteenth century. Along the naves are the portraits of all the popes. According to tradition, when all the naves for these portraits are filled (there are only twelve left), the world will end.

Above: Water from the Castellum Acquae, a massive cistern of water to the east of Rome, passed through eleven aqueducts outside the city; here they were fed into smaller pipes to supply the city. This gate, which is part of the Aurelian Wall, is one of the most beautiful in Rome. It was erected in 272 by the emperor Aurelian himself. In 1838 a curious tomb was found here, with breadlike, swirling decorations. It was built for Eurysaces, who earned his fortune by supplying half of the daily bread to the republic.

Right: Today Porta Maggiore is a connecting point to the densely populated quarters of Prenestina and Casilina, and to the University La Sapienza. Nearby is the St. Lorenzo quarter, which was bombed by Allied airplanes during World War II; of all the churches in the area, only St. Lorenzo was badly damaged. These days the district enjoys a lively nightlife and is very popular with local university students.

Bridge Milvio is, along with the Fabricius Bridge at Tiber Island, one of the oldest in Rome. It was built in 109 BC and restored in 1805 by the architect Valadier. Valadier demolished the two drawbridges that had been in existence since the sixth century but retained one of the drawbridge towers. Bridge Milvio is famous for the battle between Constantine and Maxentius, who fought to gain power in Rome in AD 312. Though Constantine was outnumbered, he won the battle, and the retreating Maxentius died here, drowned in the river after the bridge collapsed.

Houses have been built on the far side of the river, forming one of the most expensive residential areas in the city. The bridge is not far from the Foro Italico, the huge sports complex built by Mussolini. The bridge underwent major restoration after the Siege of Garibaldi in 1848–49, and in 1951, to aid its longevity, the bridge was fully pedestrianized. In most cities a bridge that is over 2,100 years old would be a highlight, but in Rome, surrounded by so much antiquity, it is sometimes overlooked. On the first Sunday of each month, an antique market specializing in pipes, pens, and other curiosities is held here.

This 1911 photograph shows a rare view of the Porta Latina, which had been walled up since 1827. In front of the gate is the small, octagonal Chapel of San Giovanni in Oleo, literally "St. John in Oil," attributed to Bramante or Borromini. It commemorates the place where the emperor Domitian plunged the disciple John into a cauldron of boiling oil as part of his persecution of Christians. Because he emerged unscathed, the Romans believed him to have magical powers and sent him into exile on the island of Pathmos, where he finally died in AD 100.

Opened again in 1911, the area surrounding the Porta Latina retains all its fascination. Nearby is the *columbarium* (vault) of Pomponius Hylas; further on is the Renaissance house of Cardinal Bessarione. St. John in Oleo is in great demand for weddings because of its twelfth-century charm and the nearby Parco degli Scipioni, a park that has become a popular place for picnickers and families.

The Porta St. Sebastian was originally called the Porta Appia because of its position at the head of the Appian Way. It was dedicated to St. Sebastian, an officer in the Praetorian guard who became a Christian, much to the anger of his emperor, Diocletian. He was ordered to be killed by archers, a fate that left him riddled with arrows but still alive. He was subsequently beaten to death by soldiers. The arch in front of the gate, the Arch of Druso, was part of the aqueduct built by Emperor Caracalla to feed his baths.

Right: The customhouses were demolished when Rome was annexed to Italy. Within the porta, the two towers, and the wall itself is a museum of the Aurelian Wall. It is possible to walk along the wall to see the astonishing views that its elevation brings. It is one of the longest walls in Europe, eleven miles in length and with 383 towers. The Appian Way makes a pleasant excursion outside the city, especially on Sundays, when the road is closed to vehicle traffic.

The Appian Way leads to the Castelli Romani, the name given to the thirteen villages located in the Alban Hills, twelve miles to the southeast of the city and famous for their wine and lakes. In this picture, *carrettos del vino* (special carts for wine) are shown; the horse is decorated with special feathers. In the background is the Aqueduct of Claudius, begun by his nephew Caligula in AD 38 and, after Caligula's death in 41, completed by his uncle between 47 and 52. It was the most important aqueduct in Rome and was over forty miles long. After only ten years, the supply failed and was interrupted for nine years, until Emperor Vespasian restored it in 71. For centuries afterward, it required constant repair.

After the aqueducts were cut by the Goths, Rome was left with just the Aqua Virgo, which ran entirely underground. One or two were later restored and used during the Middle Ages, but the majority of the people had to resort to the Tiber as their source of water. This is why the medieval buildings of Rome lie almost exclusively in the two great bends of the river, the Campo Marzio and the Trastevere. It was not until Renaissance times that the city was once again supplied by aqueducts and could indulge in the luxury of fountains. This part of the aqueduct is visible on the way to the Ciampino Airport, the second airport of Rome, which caters mostly to charter flights. The site is now an archery center.

PAY A VISIT TO
SANGIORGIs GREAT GALLERY
(Borghese Palace)
PERMANENT EXHIBITION
OF FINE ARTS

The circular building, shown here in 1920, is the best-preserved tomb on the Appian Way, the first road of the 50,000-mile Roman road system, which was constructed in the fourth century BC. This impressive tomb was built for Cecilia Metella, the beloved daughter of Crassus, who made his money by buying the burned-out properties of the poor. The tomb was later used as a medieval fortress by the Caetani family. Like most of the consular roads outside Rome, over the centuries it became lined with the cemeteries and mausoleums of the wealthy because ancient practice prohibited any burials within the sacred ground of the city itself. Spartacus led a revolt in AD 73 that lasted two years. Seventy thousand slaves rampaged through southern Italy, but they were eventually defeated and 6,000 of them were crucified and left to rot along the Appian Way.

The poster on the left of the picture seen on the opposite page, an advertisement in English for the Borghese Gallery, proves that tourism has long been a Roman industry. However, when Mussolini came to power he banned the use of foreign languages in Italy, claiming that it was unpatriotic. The area is now part of the Parco Regionale dell'Appia Antica. Comprising 8,500 acres of green space, it is protected from new developments—especially those that are seen as a threat to the area's sense of antiquity.

This is the most French of the squares built from 1811 to 1824 by Valadier in a neoclassical style, which became the style of Italy after the unification. The square connects the area of Pincio Hill—from where this picture was taken—and the area around the Vatican, which was once a vast area of meadows. This piazza was the main entrance for pilgrims coming from the north to visit the tomb of St. Peter. In the past, this place was said to be the burial area of Nero, and for this reason, it was believed to be haunted by his tortured soul. It was also a place of capital executions; outside the Porta Flaminia, prostitutes and political criminals were buried in the deconsecrated land, called the Muro Torto (Crooked Wall).

Today the pedestrianized piazza is used for political speeches, concerts, and festivals. On the left, the portico of one of the twin churches can be glimpsed. Far in the distance, close to the dome of St. Peter's, is the busy district of Prati. Memorials of capital executions perpetrated by the popes are on plaques near the Porto Flaminia, which is to the right.

Fashionable and historical cafés are located in the piazza, including the Café Rosati at No. 4 and the Café Canova at No. 16, which is frequented by intellectuals and actors. Pincio Hill is best known as a romantic place to watch the sun set over the city and it's also a great place for tourists who want to take a picture of the cityscape from a high vantage point.

INDEX